WILDFIRE FROM HELL

Poetry and Prose

Tessa Glasgow

@DEADOFNIGHTPOETRY

Dedication

To my daughter, Skylan, for unknowingly being my oxygen. I hope you grow up knowing your worth and feeling nothing but love, acceptance, and the freedom to always be yourself.

To my beautiful husband, Nathaniel, for showing me a love that is sincerely unconditional and for supporting and believing in me always.

To my parents, for all the positive changes they have made in their lives and for every little thing they do for me and my family.

To my sisters, Leigha and Monica, for being my best friends. You both have always had my back and I'll always have yours.

I love you all with my whole heart.

Table of Contents

Chapter 1: BROKEN AND BRUISED

*Trigger Warning for narcissistic abuse

FERAL LOVE

PUTRID TRUTH

SCARE TATICS

EMOTIONAL MANIPULATION

LETTER ON MY LIDS

NO VACANCY

FOUNTAIN OF FALSEHOOD

FOOL

INVERTED VOLCANO

ENERGY EATER

@DEADOFNIGHTPOETRY

Chapter 2: INNER DEMONS

FACELESS CREATURES

PUPPET MASTER

IRRITATION FLOATS

MADDENED SLUDGE

CACHE OF EMOTIONS

CHRONIC MIGRAINES

COLD BLOODED

DIVERGENT BRAIN

PAIN CLINGS

HEAT RISES

HAGGARD EYES

MISANTHROPIC MALAISE

MISSILES MISSFIRE

CLOSING SKULL

WILDFIRE FROM HELL

Chapter 3: FAMILY AND REALISTIC LOVE

A WOMAN'S LOVE

BREAKTHROUGH

FAKE IT

CRASH TEST DUMMY

LADDER

SHADOWS COWER

THE MESSAGE

RIVERS

MY SHADOWS ANTIDOTE

MY SAVIOR

LOVE DOESN'T MOVE MOUNTAINS

ROMANTICIZED BULLSHIT

SHAMING HALOS

REINFORCED HEART

LOVES WEIGHT

DANCING ON LEAVES

MY SISTER'S EYES

EFFERVESCENT HOPE

SEARCHING FOR LIGHT

@DEADOFNIGHTPOETRY

Chapter 4: HEALING

CLEANSED

CANDY COATED ACTOR

SKINLESS ENTITY

UNATTAINABLE ART

ARTERIES OF ICE

UNBROKEN

INNER PRYE

WILDFIRE FROM HELL

Chapter 5: BADASS ATTITUDE

LIES IGNITE

WILDFIRE FROM HELL

OCEAN OF INCHES

BRAIN À LA MODE

CHOOSING IGNORANCE

HYPOCRITE

IMPOSTER

PROSTHETIC WINGS

STAGNANCY

BOLD AND BRAVE

COMPLACENT CRITICS

@DEADOFNIGHTPOETRY

Chapter 6: MISCELLANEOUS

PUPIL REFUGEE

THE BACKGROUND

GELATINOUS SPINE

WHAT SCARES ME

WE ARE WEAK

I REMEMBER

ACOUSTIC SILENCER

PEACE IN THE SHADOWS

Chapter 1

BROKEN AND BRUISED

FERAL LOVE

Even if subconsciously

You were trapping me successfully

For a while…

Because I allowed myself

To feel confined by you.

I was bound by the self-hate

You spewed all over my body

Like projectile vomit.

You spoke your insecurities into me

To split my soul open…

To watch me wither into a dust

That you could sweep

Into a corner and ignore.

Each insult that grazed

Your tongue

And ricocheted off my ear drums

Slowly possessed my thoughts…

Until I took them full on

WILDFIRE FROM HELL

As my own self-doubts.

When really,

They were your inadequacies

That you tried to pawn off on me.

I started hating myself too

And believing

That I couldn't do any better

Because I was "damaged goods,"

And that's exactly

What you wanted me to feel.

That's exactly what you

Told me repeatedly.

But your love wasn't love,

No matter how hard

You tried to sell it as such.

Your love was feral.

Your love was a wild animal

Escaped from years in captivity.

Vicious.

Aggressive.

Unpredictable…

Not capable of coexisting

With affection.

Maybe that's why you tried

To cage me in with you.

Maybe I was the toy

Cowering at your feet

Meant to soothe your tameless growls.

Something to claw at.

Bite at.

Drag around.

A temporary distraction

From your inner turmoil.

You wore me down

Into a blank stare.

A hollowed cadaver.

A disgraced negative space.

But after all that time criticized

I finally realized…

It wasn't me that you hated.

You hated that you could see in me

What you couldn't see in yourself.

And I stopped letting you change me

By standing my ground.

WILDFIRE FROM HELL

Until I eventually became

That padlocked door on my cage…

Kicked in.

Unhinged.

And free from your plague.

PUTRID TRUTH

You reflect in my memory

Like a tree line in a pond…

Picturesque

And beautiful in photographs

From far away,

But nauseatingly inapt up close.

Your once soothing surface

Ripples through my lobes

As sweet beginnings

That are now impaired

With irreconcilable resentment.

Because what you failed to reveal

In the beginning,

Were the gallons of slime

Sunken and settled

On your algae blanketed depths

That distorted your insides.

I don't only blame you though

WILDFIRE FROM HELL

For fooling me

With your charming exterior.

An illusion like you

Was manmade

And hand crafted

Into this isolated depression

Incapable of sustaining life.

Your dock was already rotting

Years before we met.

Its foundation was fucked

From your very first breath.

And even though I tried

To stock you full of warm vitality…

Every ounce I invested in you died

Before my giving eyes,

Killing parts of my soul

That I may never recover.

But someday you will pay.

The decay of your underbelly

Will rise to the surface

And you'll wear the decomposition

Across your skin

@DEADOFNIGHTPOETRY

And the pleasant façade you sell

Will be spoiled by the stench

Of your putrid truth.

WILDFIRE FROM HELL

SCARE TACTICS

What I felt for you

Was not love,

But a deep desperation

To have it.

Even if that meant

Ignoring the red flags

That waved in the breath

Of your every word.

I wanted to be seen by eyes

That made me feel worthwhile,

Even if they were a little crazy.

Because for so long

I felt alone, empty, and unlovable.

You were a quick escape

From a home that broke me,

Even if only temporarily.

And what you felt for me

Wasn't love either,

@DEADOFNIGHTPOETRY

But a deep desperation

To feel like you had control

Over something in your life

Of repeated failures.

You just wanted to win the prize

Straddling the line of your lies…

I had a foot on either side

And I was leaning

In the other direction.

A challenge.

I already had a sickness

Living in my veins

That craved affection

Before you came along

And injected me with your virus,

Accelerating its growth.

And once you won my "love,"

You held onto it

With more than just hands,

But with fear,

Manipulation,

And scare tactics.

WILDFIRE FROM HELL

You promised to paint

Our walls

With my brain,

So terror would keep me chained

And I refused to take advice

From anyone else in my life.

But I finally realized

Everyone was right

When we got into our last fight,

And you grabbed a knife

Wearing the look of murder

In your eyes…

I really thought

I was going to lose my life.

But you stopped approaching me,

Seething with heat

And psycho written

Across your teeth,

To slit both of your wrists

While you cried

And survived.

So why am I the one

Who died so much inside?

You had no intentions

Of committing suicide.

You just wanted

To scare me into sympathy

So I'd stay.

And it's not fucking fair

That now I'm the one

Living with the anxiety

That everyone I hurt

Is going to kill themselves.

Everyone I disappoint

Is going to self-slaughter.

Everyone I leave

Will want to hang.

To shoot.

To slice.

To kill.

WILDFIRE FROM HELL

EMOTIONAL MANIPULATION

I picked him up

From the hospital,

Wrists bandaged tight,

Five days after

He tried to take his life.

"I'm sorry honey,

I didn't really want to die.

I just can't live without you.

Have you changed your mind?"

I fucking sympathized.

Hell, I even cried.

But ultimately,

I had to say goodbye.

His next move

Was to get my name tattooed

Where bare flesh

Meets the eye,

"You can't leave me now…

You're a prisoner

@DEADOFNIGHTPOETRY

On my skin,"

He growled.

His emotional manipulation

Left me feeling guilty

And confused.

This was over

But he refused

To loosen the noose

And I was stumbling

On his mental abuse.

But I only had myself to blame

For all the fear and pain,

Because I turned a blind eye

And chose to stay involved

With this guy

Instead of taking

My loved one's advice.

I really wish I would have listened

To all the warnings sooner,

Because then I wouldn't be

So god damn haunted

By all these fucked up memories.

WILDFIRE FROM HELL

LETTER ON MY LIDS

Carved into the concrete walls

Of my catacomb thoughts

Is what I would say to you

If my brain weren't in knots.

I've written you a letter,

One you'll never get to see.

The words aren't tangible,

They're living inside of me.

I'd destroy it if I could,

But I'm not ready to die.

It only hurts to read it

Every time I close my eyes.

@DEADOFNIGHTPOETRY

NO VACANCY

You've been rubbing horns

With my demons

And fraternizing with their sins,

Breathing on the same embers,

Triggering a friction fire within.

Be careful what you do next

Or become a hostage with them,

Because my demons aren't releasable,

They're imprisoned within my grin.

I've tried to spit them up,

But they sink talons into my chin

And I'm running out of vacancy…

There's no room to move you in.

WILDFIRE FROM HELL

FOUNTAIN OF FALSEHOOD

You were a fountain

Of insincere hope,

Eating everyone's dreams

Who tossed

Pennies of promise

Into your wishing well.

And unfortunately,

I was one

Of the hopeful.

Your misery craved

Communal camaraderie

In order to feed

Your dastard malady.

You held each

Token of faith under water,

Gloating as they flailed

And suffocated

Under your blasphemy.

@DEADOFNIGHTPOETRY

Heads up was supposed

To bring good luck,

But you made it seem

That I only threw tails,

Because you damned

My aspirations

And made me feel small.

But most of all

You took from me

The change I needed

To afford myself

The bravery to leave sooner.

So, I panhandled for praise

In all the wrong ways

From everyone else,

Until I saved enough confidence

To support myself.

And when it comes to you

And nourishing your hunger

To hinder happiness…

I pray that it's only you

Who is drowning now.

                                        WILDFIRE FROM HELL

FOOL

Your mouth shields a sword

That cuts with no remorse.

Unsheathed,

It severs everything

Into feeble fragments

Smaller than you.

It chops everyone down

One word at a time,

Making you feel big.

Powerful.

Mighty.

But you're the fool

Who lives with a scalpel

Cracking at the back

Of your teeth.

Who lives with a knife

Shredding at your gums.

No wonder you're such a cunt.

@DEADOFNIGHTPOETRY

Bite the damn blade.

Break your fucking teeth.

I'd love to watch you bleed.

WILDFIRE FROM HELL

INVERTED VOLCANO

Over the years

My pillow inflated

In the weight

Of degrading tears,

Until it was too tall

To rest my head upon,

Because I spent so many nights

Crying myself to sleep

After you tore into me

For not being enough.

Not pretty enough.

Not skinny enough.

Not interesting enough.

I slowly sank into myself

Like an inverted volcano,

Filled with your blistering hot ridicule.

I allowed myself to smolder

For so long

@DEADOFNIGHTPOETRY

That my vision blurred

And I saw you

As good enough for me.

You were a mirage that formed

From being force fed deceit.

You were so consumed

With yourself

That you fed the fire

Just to keep me fighting it.

To keep me occupied

And out of your way.

Because you didn't care

If I was withering

Into desertedness,

As long as you

Could still use me.

You didn't love me,

I was an accessory

That you could sometimes fuck

Then return to your normality

Of beating me verbally.

But I didn't love you either.

                          WILDFIRE FROM HELL

I hated your existence

And I overstayed

For one reason…

Ten tiny fingers

And toes

That I never wanted

To divide up.

It's a shame

I let you get to me.

It's a shame

I let you take parts of me

To feed your narcissism,

When I should have

Just let you starve.

@DEADOFNIGHTPOETRY

ENERGY EATER

The soft skin

Of my caring hands

Calloused into indifference

From soothing your abrasive energy.

It became so big and foreboding

That I could no longer

Wrap my arms around it

To hush its negativity.

It filled every crack

And crevasse of the room,

Like a shadow creeping

Across the walls at sundown.

It pressed me into the grains

Of our hardwood floors,

Where I became the new stain,

Drained and drowning in your existence.

You required so much fuel

And I just didn't have enough

WILDFIRE FROM HELL

To keep gassing you up.

Chapter 2:
INNER DEMONS

FACELESS CREATURES

I am haunted

By the taunting voices

Echoing inside my walls…

From the people…

The people who live

Under my skin.

It undulates

Like a pair

Of asthmatic lungs

Writhing for oxygen.

It ripples

Like enraged ocean waves

Clawing at the shore.

I can feel them crawling

From their nests

In my scars…

Strumming my veins…

Pulling at my tendons

@DEADOFNIGHTPOETRY

Like a melancholic guitar…

Making me a puppet…

Bending me at their will…

Infiltrating my brain

And playing horror reels on repeat

To remind me

How they got inside

In the first place.

I am nicotine

To these fiends

And they are addicted

To disintegrating me

With their infestation

Of past monstrosities.

These faceless creatures

Strive to own my body.

Pilot me fully.

Their gangrene essence

Escapes from my pores

In waves of irritability.

Of discontent.

But I won't give myself up.

WILDFIRE FROM HELL

I battle them daily

And one by one

I exorcise these beings.

I evict their disease.

And I will keep on fighting

Until my skin

Lays motionless

And my scars finally

Rest in vacancy.

PUPPET MASTER

They tell me I have control

Over my body

And I laugh

In their able-bodied faces,

Because they can't see his invisibility

Taking a free ride

Inside of me.

The fucking beast.

My phantom conjoined twin.

The master who pulls my strings.

He decides my daily fate,

Because he thrusts

His razor blade claws

Into my temples

And slips his serrated thumbs

Into each of my eye sockets…

Sending shock waves

Of mind-altering pain

WILDFIRE FROM HELL

Throughout my brain

Whenever he damn well pleases.

I don't get to think.

I don't get to speak.

I don't get to live for myself

Until he decides to release me

And sometimes it takes days

To earn my freedom.

But when he retreats into quietness,

Because he's heard enough

Of my desperate pleas…

I live in fear.

Because he always comes back

When I least expect it

With those prying fingers

Ready to skull fuck me

Without consent.

@DEADOFNIGHTPOETRY

IRRITATION FLOATS

How do I make it stop…

This irritation breeding

In the back of my throat?

It's dying to catapult

Past my teeth

And scream words

Plagued in impatience.

I clinch my jaws

Until my head throbs

To keep it at bay

Because if it escaped

When it makes a lunge

Towards the tip of my tongue,

I'd have no one.

Internal tears

And silence

Drown it down

Behind restraints frown.

WILDFIRE FROM HELL

But I have become

So flooded in salt water

From holding it back

That sometimes

It floats to the surface

And scratches at the walls

In the back of my esophagus…

Just hoping I will choke

And let it out.

@DEADOFNIGHTPOETRY

MADDENED SLUDGE

I want to split myself open

And purge this maddened sludge

Polluting my body…

Weighing me down,

And holding me back.

It's overflowing from my pores

And my scowl line

Is filling to the brim

In noticeable frustration.

It's eroding the crease

Between my brows

Into a bottomless chasm.

I can't see straight.

I can't think clearly,

Because this deep-seated anger

Steers me in directions

I don't want to travel in.

A place filtered in hues of red.

WILDFIRE FROM HELL

Where I hate everybody

And everything fingers my nerves.

I'm dying to wash myself

Of this long-lived annoyance

That stalks my existence.

Ring my body out

Like a wet towel

And sew myself back together

With more patient hands.

CACHE OF EMOTIONS

I learned from a young age

To manage my emotions.

To tuck them away

In the back of my brain

And leave them there to rot

In a muted cache.

Never to be talked about.

Never to be displayed.

Addiction was my teacher

And silence was the lesson.

So, I don't know how

To express myself

In the ways that you deserve,

Even though I really want to.

I keep my feelings subdued

And my expectations low,

Because it's the only way

I know how to protect myself

WILDFIRE FROM HELL

From disappointments descend

Into depression.

I can't reach

Into those preserves

Where I am most disturbed,

Because I can't ache

If I don't allow myself to feel.

So, I choke it all down

Behind hidden frowns

And pleasantries.

But I know

This is a broken system

Of self-defense

Doomed to fail.

The build up

Is bound to overflow

And when that day comes

The only protection I'll need

Will be…

From the mess created

Only by me

And my determination

@DEADOFNIGHTPOETRY

Not to be seen.

WILDFIRE FROM HELL

CHRONIC MIGRAINES

Demons summit my spine,

Trailing their sandpaper tongues,

Scraping an irritating precursor

Of what is to come.

Beads of sweat collect

As their hot breath lingers

On my neck,

Like suffocating coals

Reigniting in the wind,

Just when you think they're gone.

They gnash at my nerves,

Clutch at my clavicles,

Until it is agony

To turn my head

In any direction but down.

Their horns pierce

My welling eye sockets,

Blending my brain

@DEADOFNIGHTPOETRY

Into a state of disdain.

I have tried to exorcise them.

With pills.

With pleas.

But this is all they know

And I am their disease.

They will live

And die inside of me,

Because we are bound by genes

That will never allow me

To break free.

But other than being born

Into a fucked up family chain…

What the hell did I do

To deserve this chronic pain?

WILDFIRE FROM HELL

COLD BLOODED

I wish the ice in my veins

Would accumulate in my brain

To subdue this fucking pain.

My nerves are frayed

And I am afraid

They will continue to degrade…

And I won't want to do this anymore.

@DEADOFNIGHTPOETRY

DIVERGENT BRAIN

My brain has diverged

Into two entities

That are enemies

Occupying the same home

Within me.

The light and the dark.

The good and the evil.

The left…

A confidant trusted

With my deepest thoughts.

A cheerleader brainwashed

In optimism,

Sprinkled in certainty.

Rooting me on.

Reassuring.

My best fucking friend.

Oh, but the right.

The fucking right…

WILDFIRE FROM HELL

Is a frigid breath crawling down

The back of my neck,

Freezing me in limbo.

The white flag of surrender

Telling me to give the fuck up.

Reiterating every bad thought

I have ever had

On repeat.

Right…

Right is my own haunting.

Its wicked voice echoes

Like barrenness under my skull.

Right might just be

My biggest adversary

And simultaneously

The only sane

Part of me.

@DEADOFNIGHTPOETRY

PAIN CLINGS

Pain clings to me

As I hang from

The cliff edge of release

And repeat to myself,

"This is only temporary."

I refuse to let go.

I refuse to fall helplessly

Into the Reaper's arms

To sleep in peace eternally.

This won't last forever.

I know it never does.

So, I can't release my clutch

On the fringes of reality,

Even when it feels like

It would be much easier.

And so, I hang,

Claws deep in the ledge,

Fingertips raw and red,

WILDFIRE FROM HELL

To show suffering

That I'm the strongest bitch,

It has ever fucking fed.

HEAT RISES

The sun does seep

Through the cracks

Of my coal painted walls

Every single day

No matter how unbelievable

That may seem.

I feel its warmth.

I bask in its embrace

As it heats up my bones,

And boils my marrow

Into a warm,

Welcome home soup.

Sometimes,

I even let it stay

For a while.

Its rays paint smiles

And whimsy

Across my face.

WILDFIRE FROM HELL

But heat,

It rises every night

Without fail

And with it floats away

My state of temporary content.

Somedays though,

I cover the cracks

In sheets of stubbornness

And hide from the beams,

Restricting myself

From feeling

Anything at all.

HAGGARD EYES

These bags in tow

Under tired eyes

Are packed carefully

So no one sees what's inside.

I can't let my secrets weep

And cascade down my cheeks…

But my baggage keeps expanding

And the seams want to leak.

My eyes curse at me,

As they billow full of luggage

And I'm going to have no choice

But to expose my troubles.

WILDFIRE FROM HELL

MISANTHROPIC MALAISE

Sadness falls over me,

Like pollen in the spring

And I can't breathe.

A sinkhole opens in my chest

And sucks me into myself,

Folding me into the dark recesses

Of my emotions

Or lack thereof,

Emotions that can only

Be described as hollow.

I am numb

In these moments

That sometimes

Turn into days

Of staring into oblivion.

Every movement feels

Like a dead-end job

That I don't get paid enough

@DEADOFNIGHTPOETRY

To be at.

I am trudging through mud

That sometimes I wish

Would swallow me whole.

I am falling

From biting cliff edges,

Stomach in my throat

And I don't know

Where I'm going to land

Or if I even want to.

These moments will pass

And I will be okay,

But today is one

Of those days

Where I could get lost

In life's maze

Of misanthropic malaise.

WILDFIRE FROM HELL

MISSILES MISFIRE

Pieces of me

Will float for eternity

In deep-seated warships

Embedded on the oceanic floor

Of my salted memories.

Guided missiles misfire

And I'd be a liar

If I didn't say

That they violate

My sense of security.

I lose myself

And I feel helpless

When fragmented

Parts of me

Ascend to the surface,

Treading water

And reliving disturbance.

Inhaling and wailing.

Reminding and shouting.

It's like apparently

My daily destiny

Is merely surviving

Just inches from drowning.

WILDFIRE FROM HELL

CLOSING SKULL

I get in this weird headspace

That feels overcrowded,

Yet lonely.

It's like my head is in a vice

And my skull is closing in,

Making my thoughts panic

And spin even faster,

Making my demons

Over enunciate their laughter.

They take center stage

When I'm feeling most caged,

To prod and poke

At a brain

Already close to insane.

And there's no room

To let anyone in

To help push them off-kilter.

I'm on my own,

@DEADOFNIGHTPOETRY

Six feet under

Anxieties tombstone.

Pushing back against

Becoming completely confined

In a coffin sealed shut

With my own fucking mind.

WILDFIRE FROM HELL

Chapter 3: FAMILY AND REALISTIC LOVE

A WOMAN'S LOVE

You've become a barren home

Overgrown with prying vines,

Strangling your collapsing neck

And infiltrating your veins.

You can't catch a breath.

The air has gone stale

In your hollow,

Boarded up house…

Haunted by the visions of regret

That lurk in the overcast shadows

Of your memories.

Irreparable cracks

In your fortification

Leak warm rains…

Flooding your foundation

In puddles of sorrow

That persistence has mildewed.

Your welcome mat

WILDFIRE FROM HELL

Has faded concurrently

With your cadaverous exterior.

Winds echo through lonely rooms

That once held warmth and laughter.

A sound that used to reverberate

From deep within your bones…

Back when she made

This house a home.

You once smelled

Of freshly baked brownies

And expensive candles,

Wet coats of paint

And burning aspirations.

You were open

And inviting.

You were charming

And alive.

She was your blood supply.

But you stopped telling her

And let years pass by,

Taking her love for granted.

And when it was her time,

Your broken heart realized

A little too late

That it was always her

Who made your house a home.

WILDFIRE FROM HELL

BREAKTHROUGH

When I solved

The jigsaw puzzle of you,

Not a single piece was missing,

But the picture was askew.

A lifetime of brainwashing

Left you warped and confused.

You didn't know who you were,

You'd always been told what to do.

I dismantled the groomed image

And scrubbed away at the views,

Revealing your true nature

And beliefs that were finally you.

Reassembling the pieces,

They fit together like new.

You fell in love with your real portrait

And your self-discovery breakthrough.

@DEADOFNIGHTPOETRY

FAKE IT

Slurs disappointed me,

Twisted my insides

Into a tangled mess,

Coiled back vomit

Into my chest

And made me sink

Into myself

In disgust.

My future could wait.

I couldn't leave my sisters home

To drown in a sinking ship.

They needed me,

The peacemaker,

To sail them through

Those starless nights

Fueled by liquor

And lack of self-control.

The nights dark eyes disguised

WILDFIRE FROM HELL

My otherwise great mother

And morphed her

Into a human wrecking ball

That no one recognized.

But one hundred proof

Eventually pushed me out the door.

I needed the break.

I deserved the fresh air,

Even if it was riddled in guilt.

I was tired of righting the ship.

So, I left my sisters

With some advice,

For those long scary nights…

"Tell mom she's right

If she wants to fight…sympathize,

Even if it's killing you inside.

You have to be her peace,

Her voice of reason.

Lay down with her…

Anywhere,

I don't care.

Cuddle.

@DEADOFNIGHTPOETRY

Hold her like a god damn baby.

Rub her fucking hair

While she cries.

Let her blow snot

Into your shirt

And tell her nice things,

No matter how angry

You are inside; fake it.

Fake it for her.

It's going to be a long night.

It's going to be frustrating as hell.

She'll get up and down

Trying to start drama,

But you have to stay relaxed.

It's imperative.

Continue the routine.

Rub her hair some more.

Sing her a lullaby.

She'll eventually fall asleep

And you'll be free.

But please

Don't fuel the fire,

WILDFIRE FROM HELL

Because that fire leads

To phone cords around her neck,

Knifes against her chest

And suicide threats.

And please don't cling

To her promises.

They'll only make you lose hope.

They do not mean anything,

But she really can't help it.

She wants to heal for us.

She loves us.

Her intentions are pure.

Her heart is gold.

But addiction

Is the worst form

Of demonic possession

And she is not

The one in control."

CRASH TEST DUMMY

Her timeline just didn't look like mine,

Because I wanted her back

When I was seven, eight and nine,

Craving more attention

And starving for her time.

I wanted her back

When I was a teenager

Needing more discipline.

I needed her to be a mother,

Not another friend.

I would pray tearfully,

Gut nauseated,

Chest weighted,

Every night for decades

With no reprieve.

No relief.

No change.

So, I lost my faith…

WILDFIRE FROM HELL

In her

And in god

And his "mysterious" ways.

But here she is today,

Years after I stopped pleading,

Decades into my life,

Sober and bright.

And I would be her learning curve

All over again.

I would go back

To be her crash test dummy

Without question once more…

If that meant my daughter,

Niece and nephew

Got the exemplary grandma

She is today.

I'd be her lab rat more valiantly,

If that meant my sisters and I

Got the above and beyond mother

She freed

When she escaped the grips

Of addictions greed.

@DEADOFNIGHTPOETRY

*Mom, I am in awe of all that you have overcome. You have always been a loving mother, you just struggled with one scary ass demon. I am grateful for your strength and determination to be the best grandma and mother anyone could ask for. You should be so proud of yourself, I certainly am. I love you.

WILDFIRE FROM HELL

LADDER

I definitely felt the "step"

In stepdad growing up,

Because we both tripped

Over it repeatedly

With bruised knees

And egos too big

For our bodies.

Perhaps you always resented me

For doing better

Than your biological children,

Who made parts of your life

A complete living hell.

Maybe you resented me

Because I held so much

Of my mother's heart

And you wanted it

All to yourself.

You were really selfish with it.

You could have resented me,

Because I looked so much

Like my dad,

The first man

To steal my mother's hand.

I certainly admit

That I resented you

For hoarding her nights

And robbing me

Of the precious

One on one time

That I craved.

I certainly admit

That I resented you

For not treating me

Like I was your own.

I sometimes felt

Like an outsider

In my own home.

And I definitely resented you

For all the drama,

Arguments and yelling

That I always seemed

WILDFIRE FROM HELL

To be dragged into so young.

I sometimes felt

Like we hated each other.

That we were two fighters

On opposite teams.

But I'm an adult now,

With a child of my own

And I see things a little differently.

I look back and realize

How you showed me love

In your own little ways.

It was wrapped

In all my favorite little snacks

That you always made sure I had.

It was in the lunches

You packed me for work

Every morning

When I was old enough

To do it for myself.

It was in the tears you cried

At my high school graduation.

It was in the fights

You started with boys

That I was dating,

Because you already knew

They weren't good enough for me.

It was in always making sure

I was well fed

And in Kentucky Kingdom season passes.

It was in all the little things

You picked up for my unborn baby

When you found out

That I was pregnant.

It was in the assertiveness with nurses

When I was in labor,

Because they wouldn't listen

To anyone else about my pain.

It was in you seeing me

In my newborn baby's face

And realizing

That you had the opportunity

To love me all over again,

But much better this time.

It's in watching you

WILDFIRE FROM HELL

Be the sweetest papaw

To a little girl

Who thinks the world revolves around you.

It was in the pride on your face

Giving me away

On my wedding day.

As these years have unfolded,

The "step" between us

Has crumbled away

And you've become my ladder.

A man I can count on

To always help me reach higher.

When it comes to redemption,

You've been redeemed…

You're one of the greatest gifts

I have ever received.

@DEADOFNIGHTPOETRY

SHADOWS COWER

I find flickers of light

In my abysmal darkness,

Like spring fireflies

Flaming indigo night skies,

When you take the time

To pry demon talons

From my glazed over eyes.

And when I can see

Those sparks of adoration

Illuminating our connection,

The shadows cower

In my once dark perception.

WILDFIRE FROM HELL

THE MESSAGE

I am the message bleeding out

On wet paper,

Lost at sea

In a broken glass bottle,

Taking on water slowly.

I'm suffocating under one wave

And breathing on top of the next.

Undulating.

Tossing and turning.

Seasick.

Desperate and yearning.

But I will not sink in defeat,

As salt saturates me.

I cannot lose my buoyancy,

Even if I kind of want to.

Because when I breathe

On the crest of rocky seas,

I'm doing it for you.

@DEADOFNIGHTPOETRY

RIVERS

We are like rivers

That erode their homes,

Carving out deep,

Permanent trenches

And forging forks

Along the paths

Of least resistance.

And though we are family

Bonded by the same iron rivulets,

We are not bound by them.

So, let's take some advice

From mother nature

And go our separate ways.

DNA means absolutely nothing

When it hurts to stay.

WILDFIRE FROM HELL

MY SHADOWS ANTIDOTE

His eyes were orbs of light

Surrounded in my darkness

And even though I never meant to,

I eclipsed them sometimes…

Shadowing his shine.

And I realized over time,

Through sleepless nights

Restless with guilt,

That the parts of me

That dimmed him,

Were parts haunted by the past

And scared to death

Of vulnerability…

Of his tenderness

And untainted love.

So, I dissected myself

From the inside out,

Trying to help

Keep his eyes bright.

And it's taking some time to decode,

But I'll never stop searching

For my shadows antidote.

WILDFIRE FROM HELL

MY SAVIOR

You found me

Scattered at your feet,

Not looking for the savior

That you decided to be.

You picked me up

In warm-hearted hands

And mended me together,

Until I could stand.

But every now and again,

A piece of me breaks loose

And you never shame me

For coming unglued.

You could paint my flaws in red,

But that just isn't you.

You've never yelled out in reaction

Or dripped your bleeding wounds.

You don't deserve the cut

Of my serrated soul,

But you guide me back in place

And want to see me whole.

You say you aren't an artist

But I would disagree,

The proof is in the cracks

That you have patched in me.

WILDFIRE FROM HELL

LOVE DOESN'T MOVE MOUTAINS

Your love doesn't move mountains.

That's ridiculous.

That's the easy route.

Your love doesn't pick up

And remove obstacles.

It pushes through them,

Conquering the peaks…

Careful of falling rocks

And unsteady feet.

Your love descends

From the summit,

Bloody knuckled

And fatigued,

But victorious

And strengthened.

Destined to succeed.

@DEADOFNIGHTPOETRY

ROMANTICIZED BULLSHIT

You don't give me butterflies.

You don't catapult my nerves

Into a senseless high.

That's some romanticized,

Infatuated,

Puppy love bullshit.

But…

You do give me a warmth.

A comfort in my chest.

A safety net

And the security to be me.

You don't make me weak

In the knees.

You give me the stability I need

To stand firmly on two feet

And that is far more beautiful

Than any butterflies I've ever seen.

WILDFIRE FROM HELL

SHAMING HALOS

There's a sight more enchanting

Than heavens pearly gates,

But it isn't a fairytale,

It's painted across your face.

That one-hundred-watt smile

Puts lambent halos to shame.

Oh, that angelic grin

And the devils it could tame.

@DEADOFNIGHTPOETRY

REINFORCED HEART

You give my heart a heaviness

In the most secure way.

You have plated it in gold

And stuffed it with bouquets.

Tungsten metal

Lines the inner chambers.

You've reinforced its walls,

Protecting it from dangers.

My heart gains substance

With all that you do,

In pounds of your love,

And all that we've been through.

Holding your quirks,

It beats even stronger.

It keeps me grounded,

Being your daughter.

My heart cherishes

Your laughter and highs.

WILDFIRE FROM HELL

My heart is inscribed

With your words of advice.

I'll always be grateful

For the anchor you've gifted.

I am weighted with your love,

Yet my spirit is lifted.

@DEADOFNIGHTPOETRY

LOVES WEIGHT

You placed life's

Most valuable possession,

Your delicate heart,

In the palms of my calloused hands

And it only felt like an added weight

On my shoulders.

Why would you leave

This delicate thing

In the care

Of a disaster like me?

It feels like pressure,

Like responsibility…

Having your happiness,

Your life,

Depend on me

And my tornado personality.

It's simultaneously

A burden and a blessing

WILDFIRE FROM HELL

Having your vulnerability

Bleeding in my hands.

But I will hang on tight,

While giving it room to beat.

Just know,

That I can't guarantee

That I will bring it no harm,

Because even though I mean well,

I am as clumsy as they come.

@DEADOFNIGHTPOETRY

DANCING ON LEAVES

Her giggles saturate

The changing autumn air

As our banter sails

To unknown destinations,

Falling on nameless ears.

Leaves crunch one by one

Beneath our dancing feet.

Crunch. Crunch. Crunch.

We laugh wildly

As we skip,

Hand in hand,

To the next fallen comrade,

Browning on the sidewalk,

Waiting to be stomped.

We make falls music

With our leaps.

Making a scene.

Creating a memory.

WILDFIRE FROM HELL

Stranger's stare,

But we don't care.

Perhaps we'll teach them

A thing or two.

Childhood is fleeting

And as long as I am breathing,

I'll do anything

She wants me to do.

@DEADOFNIGHTPOETRY

MY SISTER'S EYES

In the eyes of my sisters

I am a voice

When they are rendered speechless

By life's uncertainties.

I am a best friend,

Who will give anything,

When they are in need.

I am a lifeline,

When they need

An extra set of lungs to breathe.

I am a protector,

A fortress of strength,

When they're feeling weak.

I am a comedian,

When laughter

Is the medicine they need.

I am motherly,

When advice is what they seek.

WILDFIRE FROM HELL

I am an extra limb,

When two hands

Just aren't enough.

I am silence

When they need an ear.

I am jovial

When they deserve celebration.

In the eyes of my sisters

I am everything.

At least I hope so,

Because they are all that to me.

@DEADOFNIGHTPOETRY

EFFERVESCENT HOPE

You were an angel,

Hand crafted from the lightness of clouds…

Stitched together

In the threads

Of everlasting patience,

Warmly wrapped in life's purest light.

A gift to Earth.

A gift to me,

Even if I didn't deserve

Your buoyant presence.

You lifted everyone up

In the faithful arms

Of unconditional love,

Without even trying.

Your jovial smile

And bouncy blonde curls

Carried many of us

Through life's trials.

WILDFIRE FROM HELL

Your essence was that

Of katydids chirping

In effervescent hope.

Making their enchanting homes

Among singing fields

Of dancing flowers.

*Dedicated to my beautiful cousin, Katie.

@DEADOFNIGHTPOETRY

SEARCHING FOR LIGHT

She was a lighthouse of grace,

And a totem of faith,

Gone in the blink of an eye.

She exited the stage

With a smile on her face,

Surrounded by only love.

But now the nights are longer

And the days have faded

Into pixilated shades of grey.

That girl was summer nights

And fireflies,

The twinkle in an adoring eye

And I keep searching

For her light

To guide us through

This unexpected goodnight.

*For Katie. May your sweet soul rest in peace. I love and miss you.

WILDFIRE FROM HELL

Chapter 4:
HEALING

@DEADOFNIGHTPOETRY

CLEANSING

I smell of smoke…

Of recollections disintegrated

In flames lit

By past igniters.

I have forgiven

But I am still

Trying to forget.

Charred memories drift beyond

As ash in the wind.

Sickening gases

Dance hypnotically towards

The awaiting sky.

Trauma's embers smolder

Under the inferno

Of my determination

And I will keep fueling

This burning dismissal,

Until my mind

WILDFIRE FROM HELL

Feels avenged.

Fire after fire…

These memories

Will be cleansed.

CANDY COVERED ACTOR

Your confectionary cloak taste divine

To ignorance's sweet tooth,

But it's only a matter of time

Before you rot its innocence into decay

Like you did mine,

To mirror your insides.

I am no longer naïve

To your candy covered bullshit.

I've healed enough cavities,

After biting into your false pretense,

To never take beguiling bait again.

You can sugar coat that tongue

And still…

You will taste nothing but bitterness.

You can dip your words in honey

And still…

You will enunciate acidity.

You can wrap your bones in pretty bows

WILDFIRE FROM HELL

And still…

Your marrow will boil in rancid malignancy…

A truth that will seep through your pores

And melt your delicious façade someday,

Revealing the serpentine actor,

That has always been scheming

Underneath your sugary deception.

SKINLESS ENTITY

You took seething teeth

That only knew profanity

And sunk them into me,

Peeling the layers

Of my confidence away mercilessly.

Tooth and tongue

Stripped me undone,

Until I looked like the crazy one.

You left me exposed.

No skin,

Just bones.

I became so cold,

Nervous

And

Alone…

Everything felt unwelcoming.

Laughter felt threatening.

Are they mocking me…

WILDFIRE FROM HELL

The skinless entity?

I really began to believe

That nobody liked me,

Because of the lies

You used to unsheathe

My insecurities.

But you forgot

That wounds heal stronger

Than before

And every single minute

My body was scarring

Into something better…

Something braver.

So go on honey…

Take a bite again.

It would be a sin

Not to break your teeth

On my new fucking skin.

@DEADOFNIGHTPOETRY

UNATTAINABLE ART

You were the straight-line wind

That cracked a hairline fracture

Into the window of my soul,

With the blunt force trauma

Of your cataclysmic breath.

I still stood upright,

Framed in beautiful drapes,

And performed my job,

As if my integrity wasn't compromised,

But the damage had begun.

Overtime,

You became the repeated swing

Of a sledgehammer tongue,

Splintering that fracture

Into tiny cobwebs of fragility

That fell to the floor.

You laughed and danced

Across the shattered pieces of me,

WILDFIRE FROM HELL

Bleeding out your insecurities

All over my brokenness.

I was fragmented

And useless for some time,

While you felt mighty and strong.

But your choice

To celebrate upon my decline

Afforded me the ability

To see your disease so clearly.

And my fall unleashed

The artist in me

When I hugged

My broken parts so tightly

A living mosaic materialized,

Patchworked in strength and beauty.

Now I am the mighty one

And you can't even afford a piece

From my fucking art gallery.

@DEADOFNIGHTPOETRY

ARTERIES OF ICE

Too many long nights weeping

In the aftershock

Of your defamation

Left my voice exasperated.

I became nothing

But a pathetic squeak

In the wind

To your pompous ears.

Until you finally

Went in for the kill

And slit my throat

With your switchblade tongue.

But crimson failed

To spill down

My hollowed chest,

Because any blood

I once bled for you

Ceased to pump through

WILDFIRE FROM HELL

My now artic veins.

Congealed.

Clotted.

Rotted.

You had me decaying

From the inside out.

Cold and vacant.

No feelings to be felt.

Numbed.

You were a lesson I learned

The hard way…

Love shouldn't silence me.

Love shouldn't make me weak.

So, I clutched my open neck

And staggered into freedom,

As you watched bewildered

That I had the audacity

To leave you.

Pleas and apologies

Transcended background noise

In panicked manipulation,

But they fell at my feet

@DEADOFNIGHTPOETRY

Where I stomped them

Beyond recognition.

To hell with existing

In your frigid conditions.

Outside of your apathy,

I cherished the warmth

That slowly thinned

My curdled blood

And allowed my wounds

To finally purge.

To cry.

To scab.

To heal.

WILDFIRE FROM HELL

UNBROKEN

I am a stubborn

As steel attitude.

I am shattered concrete,

Repurposed and improved.

Excavate the depths of me

To touch my fragility.

It is sheltered in a small part

Of my heart's likability,

Because the rest of me

Is fortified in durability.

I am built from bricks

Handmade by hostility…

From pistols and daggers,

Forged in fires brutality.

I am scars healed beautifully,

With a fuck you mentality.

And I will always claim victory,

When tested on my adaptability.

@DEADOFNIGHTPOETRY

INNER PYRE

I came from the bottomless buffet

Of hell's castaway land.

I have licked the soot settled between

The devil's jagged teeth

With a tongue labeled bland.

I have walked hand in hand

With corpses masked

As the living,

Inconsiderate of the rot

They were spreading.

I have littered

The grounds of purgatory

In ash polluted tears

That never eased the burn.

I have fallen at the feet

Of my horned master

And accepted the stab

Of his trident as love.

WILDFIRE FROM HELL

I have tripped

Into condemned pits

And lost fingernails

In searing hot walls

Clawing myself out

While inhaling the flames

That now smolder

In my chest.

Backbone as kindling,

I breathe fire

In my freedom now

And I can choose

To burn down the paths

Of most resistance.

Paths that lead

To places of hatred

And people of pain.

And I can choose

To cauterize those bleeding wounds

If I want to

Or I can use

My inner pyre

@DEADOFNIGHTPOETRY

To warm a deserving body…

To brighten a starless night.

It can incinerate the evidence

Of insecurities doubt.

The choice is mine,

Because I have the power now.

WILDFIRE FROM HELL

Chapter 5:
BADASS ATTITUDE

LIES IGNITE

My blood boils

When light reveals lies.

It burns through arterial walls,

Only to cool

And clot

In the back

Of my throat

And I choke

On the coagulated anger.

I cough up trust,

And curdled rage

That tastes

Like crimson coated disappointment,

A flavor I don't want

To get used to.

I will not allow myself

To be misused.

So, I tied a noose

WILDFIRE FROM HELL

Around the neck

Of your abuse

And kicked the chair

From beneath you.

I will never fall

For deceit again so easily.

You should have learned by now,

Don't ever fucking lie to me.

WILDFIRE FROM HELL

She has been burned

In the dungeons

Of Earthly purgatory…

Scorned by the screams

Of deranged demons

And choked on the dread

Of bruised egos.

She has been haunted

By the spirits

Of rabid narcissism…

Drenched in the blood

Of man's shortcomings

And drowned in the liquor

Of past possession.

She has been reduced to ashes

And sculpted into a graveyard statue

Adorning the underworld,

Charring in perdition.

She has been spit upon

And run down…

Engulfed in flames,

Savage and untamed.

She could have caved.

She should have died

And sometimes she wanted to,

But her inferno cage

Became her inspiration to rise.

She wanted to be just like it.

Indestructible and prized.

Feared and idolized.

So, she grew into a blaze

Of overdue self-rescue

And no one

Can suffocate her now.

She makes her own fucking oxygen.

She breathes life

Into her own fucking embers,

And nothing will bring her down…

Because the devil himself

Couldn't even tame

Her wildfire from hell.

WILDFIRE FROM HELL

OCEAN OF INCHES

The blank pages

Of your vanilla brain

All read the same…

Barren and empty

Of any transcendental thoughts,

Surfaced and shallow,

Programmed by robots,

Underdeveloped character,

A story with no plot…

An ocean

Of only inches,

Where drowning

Is a longshot.

@DEADOFNIGHTPOETRY

BRAIN À LA MODE

Sometimes,

I shut away my opinions

Inside the secret chambers

Of my voice box

And choose not

To speak out to you

When I know

You'll sulk and whine,

Because I don't have

The fucking patience

To deal with your decline.

But my thoughts

Are exceeding capacity

And I'm ready to explode

Into a scattered brain vomit à la mode.

An unrefined dessert

With forks for two,

I'll dig in

WILDFIRE FROM HELL

If you'll try a bite too.

Don't you grimace.

Chew. Chew. Chew.

Digesting my honesty

Looks divine on you.

CHOOSING IGNORANCE

You floated down

The false streams

Of utopian dreams

In a bubble,

Blown and sugar coated

In blissful ignorance,

Pacified in naivete,

And blinded to the real world

Spinning around you.

But reality…

It lingered

And it prowled

Like a predator camouflaged

In the underbrush,

Before it ambushed your denial

And pierced your illiterate expectations

With its rabid teeth,

Allowing honesty to invade the perforation

WILDFIRE FROM HELL

Separating your world from the real one…

Removing the veil that has kept you

So god damn oblivious

And gifting you perfect vision

That you refuse to use.

The new unfiltered view of the world

Doesn't suit your prerogative.

You call it negative.

You call it scary.

You call it ugly

And the people that live there,

You label them cynical.

But we have only ever

Called ourselves rational.

Realist

And honest.

Delusion doesn't steer our wheels here

In the real world.

Logic is our pilot

And it's time

For your first fucking flight.

HYPOCRITE

You whipped out

That tenderizer tongue,

Coated in the self-righteous

Blood of Christ,

And gave my bleeding heart

An unholy lashing.

You prayed that your god would soften

What you criticized as hard,

But you didn't know

My heart enough

To pass judgement.

You didn't care how delicate

It already was

While you bludgeoned it

With your hypocritical words.

And in the end

Your beating only made it "harder,"

And more calloused towards you.

WILDFIRE FROM HELL

You only succeeded

In losing all respect

I once held for you.

And if your god,

Who you believe

Holds the blueprints

To my being,

Sees anything

About me as defective,

Then he is not

The kind of entity

I give a shit about impressing.

@DEADOFNIGHTPOETRY

IMPOSTER

Smile that pious smile

Like your teeth

Are heavens pearly white gates

And your words

Come straight from god himself.

Put on an animated show.

Play Sunday school dress up

And pretend your walk

Is a holy parade,

Where the only candy you throw

Is laced in lies and deceit.

Preach and sermonize,

Until you have sheep feeding

From the palms

Of your seedy hands.

Those hands that strike.

Those hands that stroke.

Those hands that steal.

WILDFIRE FROM HELL

Those hands that point in judgement,

But paint holy water crosses

Across the mindless foreheads

Of your programmed herd every week.

But don't forget,

You don't fool everyone.

Some of us know you

In "real" life.

You're an imposter,

Leaning into power,

Living a falsehood…

And an exorcism

Would do you damn good.

@DEADOFNIGHTPOETRY

PROSTHETIC WINGS

I'd knock you off your pedestal,

But you'd saddle a high horse instead

And I hate to tell you honey,

But that mother fucker is inbred.

How the hell do you fly so high

With those prosthetic wings?

Do you actually believe

All the angelic shit that you sing?

You think you're so bold

And your words are brazen,

But you're more delusional

Than the praise you were raised in.

WILDFIRE FROM HELL

STAGNANCY

Life's stagnancy smells

Of musty windless air…

A humid home withered

Beyond all repairs.

It smells of mildewed basements,

With botched foundations…

Lungs coated

In rotting trepidation.

It smells of molded drywall,

Diseased beyond salvation…

Carbon monoxide poisoning

In garages unventilated.

It smells of fresh vomit

From stomachs nauseated

And like the parasitic breath

Of every asshole I've dated.

@DEADOFNIGHTPOETRY

BOLD AND BRAVE

They were raised

To dot their I's

And cross their T's,

To sit pretty and silently

In adversity…

To do what they must

To forge the peace

And usually that meant

Taking a seat.

So, they pile their dirt high

And out of sight.

They won't talk about it

And taint their lives,

But, oh, my lord,

Their rugs are rising,

No one will notice

If they keep on smiling.

They don't like each other

WILDFIRE FROM HELL

But you'd never know,

They don't let their feelings show.

But the truth is a lion

Stirring dust in the air

And she's had enough

Of their fraudulent affairs.

She's tripped on the heap

Too many times,

Exposing the grime

And voicing their crimes.

They call her a bitch

For disturbing their charades,

But if they knew honesty...

They'd call her bold and brave,

Because she's paving a way

For some fucking change.

COMPLACENT CRITICS

They whisper behind hands

As if no one can see.

It'd be a tragedy

If their daughters turned out

To be like me.

I see their faces

When I say what I want

Without reservation

And they sit disgusted, judgmental

And complacent.

How do they breathe

Through all of that huffing?

Their scowl lines deepening

And demeanors so stuffy.

They want their daughters

Meek and mild.

They want their daughters

Forcing fake smiles.

WILDFIRE FROM HELL

What a shame it would be

To be so passive aggressive.

What a shame it would be

To be so unimpressive.

@DEADOFNIGHTPOETRY

Chapter 6:

MISCELLANEOUS

WILDFIRE FROM HELL

PUPIL REFUGEE

Melancholy eclipses the light

In her story book eyes

And tries to hide behind auburn irises,

But I get glimpses of its disdain

In our mundane conversations.

It rears its solemn head

From behind onyx pupils

To feast on

The remnants of glitter

It previously left behind…

Without her even knowing

That her secret

Is making itself known.

It's a chained prisoner,

Screaming in the basement

From a house filled with horrors,

Just hoping someone

Will hear the cry for help…

@DEADOFNIGHTPOETRY

And I did.

But when I asked

If she was okay,

She lied.

She closed her eyes

And she fucking lied…

Because that's what we've been taught

To do our whole lives.

WILDFIRE FROM HELL

THE BACKGROUND

The shading of my self-portrait has faded

Into a one-dimensional black outline,

Blending seamlessly into the background

Of everyday life.

A much better highlighter

Than highlighted.

I am the obsidian sky,

Giving stars a base to shine from.

I am the once blank canvas,

Quietly holding works of tremendous art.

I am the helium gifting flight to balloons.

I am the stem hoisting blooms

On a pedestal.

I am the setting

But not the scene.

I am the lamp,

But never the bulb.

I was never meant to stand out.

@DEADOFNIGHTPOETRY

I wasn't made to catch eyes.

I'm not here to take center stage

Or sign autographs all night.

I was born

To be the dark contrast.

The backdrop.

The frame.

I am the person

That gives the brightest torches

A platform to stand out on,

In a life,

Where everyone is competing

For fortune and fame.

WILDFIRE FROM HELL

GELATINOUS SPINE

I watched you flounder through life

As if your spine were gelatinous.

You never stood up straight,

Looked anyone in the eyes

And said what was on your mind,

And I know there was a lot.

You swallowed it all in secrecy,

With shaking hands

And a trembling chin.

Your meager demeanor

And inability to say no

Allowed everyone to take advantage

Of your kindness,

And it wore on you,

Until your spine physically curved to mirror

The powerlessness you embodied.

I loved you for your beautiful heart,

But despised your inability

@DEADOFNIGHTPOETRY

To put your foot down.

There should have been a balance,

Because you deserved to stand tall and strong.

You deserved to be understood.

But I want to thank you

For showing me exactly

What I never wanted to be.

I may be loud.

I may be opinionated

And obnoxious,

But I will always

Make myself heard

And my spine…

It will never fucking curve

Under silence like yours.

WILDFIRE FROM HELL

WHAT SCARES ME

Sometimes people choose

To only see

The parts of things

That scare them.

In the darkness

They see anxiety

When they could see peace.

In the unknown

They see insecurity

When they could see adventure.

In mystery

They see uncertainty

When they could see discovery.

In adversity

They see tension

When they could see possibility.

And in death

They see the end

@DEADOFNIGHTPOETRY

When they could see intrigue.

But in the light

They always see promise,

So unwary,

And that's where I see everything

That's truly fucking scary.

WILDFIRE FROM HELL

WE ARE WEAK

Why do we need the answers

To unanswerable questions

So desperately

That we are willing to accept lies

To make ourselves feel better?

Why are our minds so vulnerable

That they allow us to believe

Impossible things as reality?

We are so easily warped,

And so effortlessly molded

Into comfortability,

And it's fucking weak.

We need to normalize

Not understanding everything,

Rather than pacifying our pathetic needs

With stories of the make believe.

@DEADOFNIGHTPOETRY

I REMEMBER

I remember when she radiated

Nothing but positivity.

When she saw the good

In everything.

When she believed

In people and humanity.

When she wanted nothing more

Than to be a light

In a world

That could use a break

From the strangle

Of responsibility,

That could use some relief

From the burden

Of treading water

To make ends meet.

I remember when she felt

Like medicine

WILDFIRE FROM HELL

For souls

That needed healing,

When she could be the wind

In slacking sails

And the push

To take a leap.

I remember

How she used to be

The heart of a party

And sometimes

I mourn the loss

Of her innocence.

I miss her blissful ignorance.

But her cup is still half full.

Of that, I am sure,

Because I am her

And she is me.

And even though life

Has clouded the water inside,

She somehow sees

Through the glass more clearly.

The world doesn't need

@DEADOFNIGHTPOETRY

Another participation trophy

Pat on the back.

It doesn't need

Another muscle memory

Inspirational quote

Retorted in adversity.

It doesn't need another band aid

Or short-term remedy.

It needs to heal the wounds

That we speak positivity into

For a temporary solution.

It needs voices

Willing to tell the hard truths

And bodies that are capable

Of making bold moves.

WILDFIRE FROM HELL

ACOUSTIC SILENCER

There's an echo reaching out

From behind your voice

That belongs to those

Who haunted your past,

And they are screaming,

Screaming of all the ways

They fucked you up.

They did you wrong

And you wear it

In your words.

These people shaped you

And your story

Needs to be heard,

But you don't deserve

To hear them speak it endlessly.

So please,

Let me be

The acoustic silencer

@DEADOFNIGHTPOETRY

That holds onto

Your terrible memories.

Let me help you bid

Their reminders adieu,

So, you can finally speak

In a tone

That belongs to only you.

WILDFIRE FROM HELL

PEACE IN THE SHADOWS

I am being held captive

In the catacombs of darkness

By untamed abductors of light

Who feed off of my demons,

But I am not hidden here

Against my will anymore,

Because I have found peace

In the shadows,

Intrigue in the obscurities,

And rest in the stillness

Of living unnoticed.

There is a beauty

In the ambiguity,

The anonymity

And the mystery

That shades my face

From the conformity

Of society.

@DEADOFNIGHTPOETRY

ABOUT THE AUTHOR

Tessa Glasgow was born on October 12th, 1986 and was raised in the mid-western United States. She grew up in a working-class family that was far from perfect. She has two sisters and is the middle child. She became a mother to her one and only child, Skylan, in 2008 and that is when she feels like her life truly began.

Tessa has weathered some tumultuous relationships, both physically and mentally, before meeting her precious husband, Nathaniel, of ten plus years, who has helped her heal. However, those past narcissistic relationships have given her plenty of material to write about and even though she is mostly healed, she continues to write about her experiences in hopes of helping others break free from similar

WILDFIRE FROM HELL

situations and begin the healing process too. She wants others to realize that they are not alone in their brokenness from abuse, whether it be physical, mental or both. She wants anyone who finds her content relatable to feel free to reach out to her if they ever need to talk.

@DEADOFNIGHTPOETRY

Contact me:

    IG: @deadofnightpoetry

    Email: deadofnightpoetry@yahoo.com

Cover art credit: @nenu_ph

WILDFIRE FROM HELL

@DEADOFNIGHTPOETRY

Made in the USA
Columbia, SC
12 October 2023